Remedy

By John Roedel

John Roedel

Remedy by John Roedel

Author Website: www.johnroedel.com

Cover photo by golden_designs1
www.fiverr.com/golden_designs1

ISBN: 9798755221047

printed in the USA

Dedicated to Sheryl Van Pelt & Cynthia Givens

Years ago, the two of you planted the acorns of poetry inside of my heart that would eventually grow to become fat elms. I am forever grateful. Thank you for being the best teachers a mouthy kid like me could have ever had. Your vocations and love have made this world a better place. For better or worse, every single word of this collection is because of you.

John Roedel

My Great-great Grandfather, Andrew Roedel, stepped off a train in Cheyenne, Wyoming in 1885. He had made his exodus from Ohio to the edge of the wild west to help his failing lungs thrive at a higher altitude and to open up a pharmacy.

I have long imagined Andrew walking through the train depot with a jar of leeches and a single brown suitcase that carried all of his worldly possessions. By all accounts, he was a very serious man, so, I think he probably was wearing a scowl on his face as he took stock over his new dust cloud town.

He opened "Roedel's Drug Store" in 1887 and it remained in our family until the big box stores finally got their kill shot against us in the summer of 2007. Four generations of our family worked, fretted, and bled the doors of Roedel's Drugstore to stay open for as long as we could.

Eventually, the future caught up with our past and the store closed under my watch in 2007.

I grew up in our store. It was my favorite school that I have ever attended. I learned about business, empathy, relationships, math, health, science and sex all from the seemingly endless aisles of Roedel's Drugstore.

My Father, Grandfather and Great-Grandfather and countless other pharmacists who worked behind the counters of our store handed out millions of prescriptions to the citizens of Cheyenne over the 120+ years we stayed open. They transcribed these slips of papers that doctors scribbled out for their ailing patients and then filled these tiny amber vials with various remedies.

When I was ten years old, I was probably one of the only boys alive who would have rather played pharmacist than war. I would wear one of my dad's old white lab coats and then open up a little makeshift pharmacy outside of my house and hand out little cups of M and M's to kind passersby who likely would throw them out when they went around the block.

I think I would have loved being a real pharmacist, however, I never had a mind for science - unless you count science fiction movies.

My brain was not suited for working in medicine. In college, I took a chemistry class where after two days I realized the professor would have more luck teaching a radish to land an airliner than it would be to impart any information to my haunted house of a brain.

I have always regretted that I never had the skill set or intellect to become a pharmacist.

I believe I would have found such purpose in helping guide a sick person through the maze of their symptoms. To work in an apothecary is to be a modern-day healer. I can't imagine a more personally fulfilling vocation than to bring people back to wellness.

My journey into writing began years ago (about the same time that our family's drug store closed for good) when I felt my heart being torn apart by an unseen grizzly bear. Every day, it seemed like more and more of my

John Roedel

life force was being consumed by this monster I didn't know had been hibernating inside of me for years.

By the time I noticed that I was suffering from depression it had already dug its roots deep inside of me. I began to believe the insidious lies of depression and found myself wondering if the world would be better off without me

At first, I would simply fantasize over how much of a relief it would be to get hit by a piece of space debris - but over time, my thoughts grew more sinister as I started imagining more realistic means to my end. I sought help the moment I caught myself staring at an extension cord plugged into my bedroom wall and wondering if it could hold the weight of my body

I started writing little tiny missives to myself to help me untangle the thick knot of my mental and emotional unwellness. Oftentimes these pieces would just be a line or two of dialogue between myself and "God" about how angry I was. Eventually, these writings evolved into just straight poetry - despite the fact that I never read a single line of it before in my adult life.

What I didn't think about until years later was that these little poems were just prescriptions that my heart was writing me. I would discover these little messy notes written on the walls of my heart that I would then spend time transcribing. Each and every poem was a balm for my unwell emotional health. As soon as I finished a poem it became a bandage for my wounded soul. These pieces were the penicillin for the abscessed infection of depression that was spreading throughout my body.

The poems included in this collection are all the prescriptions that my invisible angelic doctors wrote for me to fill for myself. I am not exaggerating when I say that without these poems, I don't think I would still be here. I am certain that I would have been consumed by the darkness.

I think of the following forty poems as little amber vials, not unlike the ones my ancestors used to hand out to customers. I hope that these words help you on your journey back to yourself. I hope you find the same healing in these poems that I found for myself.

There is no snake oil here. There is only an offer of remedy from my broken heart to yours. I guess I did become a pharmacist of sorts after all.

John Roedel

#1

my brain and
heart divorced

a decade ago

over who was
to blame about
how big of a mess
I have become

eventually,
they couldn't be
in the same room
with each other

now my head and heart
share custody of me

I stay with my brain
during the week

and my heart
gets me on weekends

they never speak to one another

- instead, they give me
the same note to pass
to each other every week

and their notes they
send to one another always
says the same thing:
This is all your fault

on Sundays

my heart complains
about how my
head has let me down
in the past

John Roedel

and on Wednesday
my head lists all
of the times my
heart has screwed
things up for me
in the future

they blame each
other for the
state of my life

there's been a lot
of yelling - and crying

so,

lately, I've been
spending a lot of
time with my gut

who serves as my
unofficial therapist

most nights, I sneak out of the
window in my ribcage

and slide down my spine
and collapse on my
gut's plush leather chair
that's always open for me

- and I just sit sit sit sit
until the sun comes up

last evening,
my gut asked me
if I was having a hard
time being caught
between my heart
and my head

John Roedel

I nodded

I said I didn't know
if I could live with
either of them anymore

"my heart is always sad about
something that happened yesterday
while my head is always worried
about something that may happen tomorrow,"
I lamented

my gut squeezed my hand

"I just can't live with
my mistakes of the past
or my anxiety about the future,"
I sighed

my gut smiled and said:

"in that case,
you should
go stay with your
lungs for a while,"

I was confused
- the look on my face gave it away

"if you are exhausted about
your heart's obsession with
the fixed past and your mind's focus
on the uncertain future
your lungs are the perfect place for you

there is no yesterday in your lungs
there is no tomorrow there either

there is only now
there is only inhale
there is only exhale
there is only this moment

John Roedel

there is only breath

and in that breath
you can rest while your
heart and head work
their relationship out."

this morning,
while my brain
was busy reading
tea leaves

and while my
heart was staring
at old photographs

I packed a little
bag and walked
to the door of
my lungs

before I could even knock
she opened the door
with a smile and as
a gust of air embraced me
she said

"what took you so long?"

John Roedel

#2

oh, my troubled lovely,
oh, my weeping daisy,
oh, my fading candle,
oh, my broken beauty,
oh, my crumbling stronghold,

stay with us
here on Earth

don't rapture yourself;
- we need you

before you decide to leave,

sit with me here in your unmade self
at the edge of your unmade bed

and listen to me
tell you one last secret

oh, my tearful songbird,

if you can find
a way to
survive long

enough

someday you'll become
the answer to somebody
else's most desperate prayer

by just being there in
the same room that they are in
- as they gently fall apart

and at that moment
you won't need to say anything

you'll just need to drape your hands

John Roedel

over theirs like a Good Friday altar cloth
until they believe in resurrection again

- that's why you can't give up

your life will someday be the rainbow
at the end of someone else's storm

if you aren't still here
when they fall off
the bridge

then who will be there to catch them?

I know it's not quite fair
- but your life isn't just yours

it also belongs to that person
who is going to need you
to be alive later

you are part of the community
of unintended angels

who has a sacred calling

of surviving your darkest night
so someday you can be the
sunrise for somebody else who
will need you to prove to them
that daybreak always returns

oh, my clouding diamond,
oh, my shaking sunflower,
oh, my doubting saint,
oh, my disappearing moon,
oh my quieting symphony

stay here
with us
on Earth

John Roedel

because if you do

you will save a dozen lives
by first saving your own

it's the great pyramid scheme
of hope

you must persist
so they can watch how you persist

turn this riptide you
are drowning under

into a ripple
of hope
that stretches
through time

that you can ride until
you reach that one moment
in your life where you'll find yourself
in a quiet room with somebody
who wants to become a shadow

and you'll be able to say to them
with authority the same thing
I am saying to you right now:

"oh my troubled lovely,
oh, my weeping daisy,
oh, my fading candle,
oh, my broken beauty,
oh my crumbling stronghold

stay with us
here on Earth

don't rapture yourself
we need you..."

John Roedel

#3

once upon a time,

an angel visited a man who
laid broken

in a thousand pieces on
his bathroom floor

the room was
so dark

and the man was
so tired

"I've come undone,"
he said

"Yes you have," the angel replied
as she held his head

in her shimmering
lap

"but," she continued
"don't be afraid

because sometimes when
we shatter

we get to become a brand
new creation

- sometimes our brokenness can
be made into art."

suddenly all of the man's numerous
fractures began to glow

- and suddenly the broken spaces
in him turned into light

John Roedel

and suddenly his scars became
feathers

- and suddenly he was rising up
off of the bathroom floor

and suddenly the darkness
never found him again

John Roedel

#4

the journey from
being wounded
to being healed

will take exactly
as long as it needs to

I know you want
to rush to get
your scar as
soon as you can

but my love,

recovery isn't meant to be a race

it's often a slow walk
down a five-mile
curvy country road

take your time
coming back
to yourself

let your repairs
happen carefully

mend your heart
like it is a cathedral
that is being
gently restored

one carefully laid
- brick
-mosaic tile
-and shard of stained glass
at a time

my love,

John Roedel

your scars will
come to you in time

and someday they will teach you
a masterclass in how strong you are

but in the meantime,

nurse your wound like a
newborn

-slowly
-thoughtfully
-and with the softest of thoughts
my love,
the sound of your heart
makes as it heals
is my most favorite psalm
don't rush through the verses
of your sacred recuperation
-let your lyrics echo
-let them linger
-let them dawdle
let them hang in the air
like fireflies
until they surround you
and help you stand on
your feet again
your comeback
starts now

however,
not with a footrace
on hard pavement

but rather, your return
to yourself will begin
with a meandering walk
down a stretching dirt path
under a cotton candy sky

my love,

John Roedel

don't set your watch
to your healing

don't give it
a deadline

instead

give it all the
time it needs

to replant the garden
of your flowering purpose

oh, my love, oh, my love,

I wish you could
see what I see

I wish you
could see
how incredibly
beautiful you
look

while you heal

John Roedel

#5

I was the last person you (or any of my past English teachers) would have ever thought would become a poet.

I started writing poetry about three years ago while suffering through a destructive tsunami of depression.

Every day I felt myself being pulled out to sea to drown in melancholy- and writing poetry was the only thing I could find to bring me back to shore.

During the worst of it (and believe me, it was truly horrible) in early June of 2016, I started a collection of poems that were just for my eyes only.

The private collection of poems I was writing was called "During This, My Last Summer on Earth."

I was fully convinced I wouldn't make it out of the summer alive.

Every day I felt as if I would just turn into ash and any trace of me would be blown away in the howling Wyoming wind.

I wrote every day to save my life - and coupled with some outside help I was (obviously) able to survive the insidious lies depression was telling me.

Each of those poems in "During This, My Last Summer on Earth." were written like a letter to myself.

I was begging myself to hang on.

I was 42 without a career or any hope of really finding one. Everything in my life was so rudderless. I was just floating along. I was waiting at a bus stop that wasn't on any route.

I couldn't stand the way my life looked. I wanted to throw up every time I was forced to contemplate the image I was giving the world.

I was a cliche.

John Roedel

All around me were successful people driving fancy cars and taking exquisite vacations - and here I was barely existing. I cursed my life. I wished I would have been born somebody else. I wished I would have been given a different brain and heart. I loathed myself completely.

It was when I wrote the following poem that a revelation came to me:

I was so obsessed with
trying to be like other people
that I started to use them as mirrors.

I was basing my success on how I compared to my friends and neighbors. I was attempting to (and failing) to form my image around how other people appeared to live their life.

I was done lying to myself.

I was ready to embrace my journey to be a unique artist. I was ready to look at my life through a gentler set of eyes.

I wrote this poem in a trance-like state. I was overcome with purpose. It was one of the first things I ever wrote where I can feel my veins burning. It was as if I had already known the words I was writing. I wasn't being creative. I was transcribing a truth I was suddenly remembering.

This poem and the other 59 that I wrote from "During This, My Last Sumner On Earth." likely saved my life.

I will probably never release any of the other ones for public consumption - but I want to share this one with you today.

I have this deep compulsion that somebody else needs to read it as I did.

****

Dear, you,
if you don't like

John Roedel

the way that you
look it's probably
because you have
chosen the wrong
mirror to look at
yourself in

stop using other people as a mirror
to see your reflection in

- especially if that other person is unkind

unkind people make the worst mirrors
they only want to reflect back on your blemishes

and your weaknesses
and your fault lines
and your sins

don't blame them for making you feel bad
you are the one looking for them
to tell you how you look

of course, they will tell you that you're ugly
of course, they will say you aren't enough

they are unkind- what did you expect?

while we are at it...
you should also
stop using your
bank account as a mirror

it's a liar
it doesn't really show
you who you really are

neither does your car
or your grades
or your awards
or your Instagram
or your past mistakes

John Roedel

or your diagnosis
or your late bills
or your failures

none of those things make very good mirrors

If you want to know how you actually look I suggest that you hold a baby for a bit.

Pay attention to how a baby will look at you. To a baby, you are a garden of a million glowing pastel moonflowers. You are a wonder. You are exotic.

To a baby, you are a giant. You are an ancient warrior protecting them from monsters and uncomfortable rashes. You fill up their sky like a brilliant supernova. You are the sky and sea.

To a baby resting in your arms, you are both the cradle and the lullaby. A baby will gaze at you with wide eyes and an uncontrollable smile because they have just come from heaven and they know divinely crafted beauty when they see it.

They see the miracle in you. They see the miracle in you. They see the miracle in you.

Babies make the best mirrors. Look at your reflection the EXACT way a baby looks at you.

For too long you have let dirty and broken shards of glass tell you who you are.

Those reflections are corrupt - stop trusting them.

Let the innocent show you who you are. They see your light. They see you for who you are:

Capable
Strong
Beautiful
Burning
Blooming
Becoming

John Roedel

in the time you have left
during this,
your last summer on Earth,

be kind to yourself
and choose what reflections
you believe with the
utmost of care.

See you in September,
you're going to make it
to see the frost kiss all
of the leaves yellow

I swear it

love,
me

John Roedel

#6

when somebody falls apart
don't try to put them back
together in your image

in fact, don't try and
to reassemble them at all

that's not your job

instead - lay on the ground with them
and scoop as many of their broken
pieces into your hands as you can

and every now and then whisper to
those pieces

"This is not forever."

that's your job

John Roedel

#7

- you are standing in the wind
but you are not of the wind

the wind is just what flows through you

- you are standing in the river
but you are not of the river

the river is just what moves around you

- you are standing in the sunlight
but you are not of the sunlight

the sunlight is just what passes through you

- you are standing in the wreckage
but you are not of the wreckage

the wreckage is just what surrounds you

- you are radiating with joy
but you are not of the joy

the joy is just what moves through you

- you are suffering from depression
but you are not of depression

depression is just what passes through you

- you are so lovely in the skin you were given
but you are not of your skin

your skin is just what surrounds you

- you are living in this hard world
but you are not of this hard word

this hard world is just what moves around you

John Roedel

my love,
everything
is in constant transition

everything that happens to you
is nomadic

the things of this world are
constantly traveling through you
but it should never become

you

a car doesn't become a part of
the tunnel it races through,
does it?

you are the great passage
where all meaningful
experiences move through

be careful of the things you cling to
or they will define you
or they will jam up the tunnel

let these things come
and let these things go

so you can allow for whatever
needs to come next
safe passage through you

be the hallow bone

- strong
-unblocked
-unburdened

nearly weightless
be the gentle pipeline
where the matters of life
move through you so

John Roedel

effortlessly to get to
wherever they need to go next

my love,
we have been wounded
but we are not of our wounds

we have been angry
but we are not of our anger

we have cried a thousand tears
but we are not of our tears

it's all a passage
of emotion and experience

it's the freeway of life

that became a mountain tunnel
welcoming invisible travelers
to pass straight through
the center of our hearts

it's all
coming and going
coming and going
coming and going going going

don't cling to any of it

keep your hands free
so I can wrap mine
in yours

because, if anything is to remain
with us after we leave this world
that we are moving through

let it just be our connection

please, oh please
let it be us

John Roedel

I may not be of
this world

but I am of you

oh, my love,
I am of you

John Roedel

#8

I lost my right eye
a day before
Easter when I was eight

it was Holy Saturday
that became my holey-eyeterday

there was this stick
that was just minding
it's own business
being a pretend wand
in the hands of
a pretend wizard
named David

and I ran right into it

pupil first

the last thing I
remember seeing
with my right eye
was David's face
as he was casting a spell
to kill an invisible orc

and then came

the indescribable pain
of my exploding lens

I passed out

when I woke up
about five minutes later
I was I sitting in
my dad's chair

that he spent
two hours a night

John Roedel

reading mystery novels in

I knew I must
have been in
bad shape if
they were letting
me sit in that chair

I could only open my
left eye

my right eye was sewn shut
with agony

my dad was talking to
me but I couldn't
quite hear what he was saying

the only thing I could focus on
was the sound of my mom
crying behind him

"Open your eye. Let me look,"
my dad said with his hands on my face

I rememeber his fingers were covered in soil

he must have been gardening
when he got the news that I
had been struck by some dark magic

I tried to open my eye
- I couldn't.

There was a monster
under my eyelid
devouring my sight

with a bit of force
my dad helped me pry
my eye open for a fat second

John Roedel

and I watched it with my
left eye how his face
turned smokestack grey

"shit..." he said

the light poured into my
right eye like lava

my right eye became fire
- and I passed out again

the next thing I remember
I was laying in the back
of my parent's white Zephyr
as they raced me to the hospital

the fresh smell of pesticide
surrounded me

it turned out that
my dad had, in fact,
been gardening

poor dad

one minute he was planting carrots at his
garden downtown

the next he was watching his son
through his rearview mirror
convulse in the back of his car

thus is the life of a parent

from turnips to tragedy
in a heartbeat

my head in my mom's lap
her hands on my forehead – shaking

my mom loved me

John Roedel

but she was never really
very physically affectionate

so, the feeling of
her hands on my head
was like a comet

rare
comforting
celestial

my nose started bleeding
and I passed out again

woke up a day later
with an eye patch
the size of Panama

it was Easter morning

but there would
be no resurrection
for my sight

the tomb of my vision still
had a stone in front of it

I was devastated - destroyed -despondent

a man in a white coat
came into my white room
with a brown clipboard
and told me even though

I had endured a
six-hour surgery
that my right eye was
destroyed

"like The Death Star?"
I asked

John Roedel

"I don't know what that is," the doctor said

I hated him for that answer

how could somebody
who dedicated their life
to the practice of science
not know what The Death Star is?

It was in that
exact moment that
I learned to never
trust a person who
was big on clipboards
but small on pop culture

since that day
before Easter
when I was eight
when I lost my right eye

the only thing
I can see are the
things that are to
the left of me

- and the things that are left of me
-and the people that have left me
- and what little time I have left

I usually couldn't see anything
right in front of me

now, 38 years later

I am left with
grey hair

-and parents who left me

- and a right eye that I am left with

John Roedel

that aches every time it rains

I was left with
the memories
of that big stick

-and of the look on David's face
-and that red chair with my dad
-and that car ride with my mom
-and that doctor
-and everything that came after

all of the good times
-and all of the bad

but here is the biggest
plot twist of it all

well, two plot twists really

1) my "good" eye is beginning to fade

and (more concerning)

2) my memories are starting to drift
away
   away
      away

a....w...a...y from me

the details of my past are starting to swirl
and fade and mist and morph

I'm losing my memories
which is terrifying for a guy who has spent
most of his life looking backward

for the man with one eye
the present has always been
my blind spot

John Roedel

- and now so is the past

I haven't been able to see
what's right in front of me

- and now I am having a
hard time seeing what's left

but here on Easter morning
despite my fading vision
and my cotton candy brain

I'm filled with hope
because there are other ways to see
the world than with just my eyes

and there are other ways to experience
the past than just with my mind

the less I see
the more beauty I'm starting to witness

the less I can remember about yesterday
the more I'm able to able to prepare for tomorrow

all of my senses are tied to my heart

it has my ears, eyes, tongue
fingers, nose and brain

everywhere I go
I'm surrounded by color

I can taste them on my lips
feel them running over my skin
hear them singing a sweet song
rising up like a bouquet in my nostrils
filling up the dark space in my blindness
overwhelming my cobwebbed memories

many years ago, I woke
up in a hospital bed on

John Roedel

Easter morning thinking
my life had ended

- really though, it had only just begun

John Roedel

#9

every single one of your scars
is a songbird

that sings the sweetest
morning song

about how you have survived
the long dark night

- don't ever be ashamed
of your scars

they are part of what makes
you so lovely

because
because, my love
because

there is nothing more
seductive than a person
who wears their scars like
midnight white-laced lingerie

- you must start looking at
yourself with kinder eyes

you are a living masterpiece of
watercolor courage

you are my favorite
piece of moving art

you have allowed your wounds
to become brushstrokes

you have become a painting who
broke out of their crooked frame

and you now walk among us

John Roedel

like a barefoot angel whose
broken wings are now on the mend

oh, my love,

don't hide your scars like
they are blemishes

they are the opposite

-your scars are your songbirds
-they are are your lingerie
-they are your brushstrokes
-they are your beauty marks

your scars are what make
you so lovely

and that's why I gasp
for air whenever you
walk into the room

because
because, my love
because

there is nothing more
breathtaking than
watching a person be
brave enough to
let themselves finally

heal

"Why haven't you quit yet?" My Depression asked me as I sat fully
clothed in my empty bathtub.

I didn't answer.

Instead, I just stared at the janky image of myself that was being
reflected back to me from the porcelain of the tub.

John Roedel

My Depression knelt down beside me and ran its thin fingers through my hair.

"Why are you resisting me?" It asked with a bit of a hiss. "I'm just here to help you feel safe."

I shook my head ever so slightly.

Subtle gestures like this were how the two of us usually communicate with each other.

However, today my Depression was being a bit more overt. Today it was motivated to destroy me. It smelled blood in the water. My Depression could see the weakness in my eyes. It knew it has a chance. If it tried hard enough - Depression thought it could finally bury me today.

With its icy breath blowing in my ear Depression spoke again with a sing-songy voice:

"It's okay, my sweets. You've already made it so much farther than anybody would have ever expected. You've endured so much suffering. It's okay to give up. Just for today try giving up. You'll feel so much better. The pain will go away. The lava in your veins will cool. The knife in your stomach will stop being twisted. The rat chewing through your heart will fall asleep. If you just give surrender you will stop feeling these holes being put in you. If you just lay with me for a bit you'll go numb. Imagine how wonderful that will be? To just be cauterized to it all? Don't you want to be done with this world? Don't you want to become an empty page? Don't you want to be safe from people who do nothing but hurt you? I can give you all of that. Stop resisting me and everything will be okay."

I shook my head again - this time a bit more forcefully. I curled up my legs tighter up against my body. I felt like a turtle hiding inside if its shell.

My Depression's long pencil-like fingers stopped moving through my hair. It pressed its face

John Roedel

up against mine. I could feel the worms move under its clammy cheek.

"Don't you want to know the peace that comes from giving up?" My Depression asked me.

I broke my silence.

"Numbness and peace aren't the same thing," I replied.

With that my Depression's tone with me quickly changed. I could feel it grip my hair and try to pull it out from my roots.

"Listen to me you little failure.," it wheezed. "You are nothing. You are broken. You are sick. You are only a disappointment to people. There is nothing you can do to get away from me. I will own you someday. You can't stop me. This is a battle that you will never win. You will never be rid of me. You are stuck with me!"

As a fat daddy tear grooved her way down the bridge of my nose and I said with a trembling voice:

"I'm stuck with you?"

Depression lips formed a frown that nearly touched the bathroom floor.

"Yes..." it said.

"If that's the case then maybe we should go get some tacos...I'm starving."

My Depression let go of my scalp and slumped down on the floor next to me and sighed loudly.

After a few minutes of silence between us, it spoke again.

"Chicken tacos?" Depression asked.

"Sure," I said as I stood up. "I know how you love them."

John Roedel

My depression and I went for an awkward lunch together. We didn't say much to each other but at one point toward the end of our meal it asked me one last question for the day:

"Why won't you just give up?"

I took a long sip from my straw and I replied with:

"I guess I'm just too curious about what comes next," I replied.

My Depression nodded ever so slightly.

Subtle gestures like this were how the two of us usually communicate with each other

John Roedel

#11

You are going
to survive this.

I swear.

Please hold on.

Oh, my love,
you will be
on the other side
of this suffering soon

I swear.
Please hold on.

John Roedel

#12

hello, I know that we just met,

but I can't help but
notice that you have
an open wound

that will not quite heal

- I'm so sorry that
happened to you

I have been hurt like
that before and I know
how an unseen cut can fester

if you let me,
maybe I can help you

feel like yourself again

- take my hand
and come with me
down to the river

- forget about everything you
think you know about what
you can handle or how
strong you are

- or about rivers

because you may
not know anything
about these things [yet]

please sit down
in the sun-kissed stream

- in a moment you will
feel the current wrap her

John Roedel

rushing hands around you
as she starts gently pulling
the thick thorns out of your
thin skin one by one

then the moving water will
wash you like a newborn

yes, it will sting
yes, it will ache

- comebacks often do

please don't leave
the stream until your
wound closes

until you are healed

don't rush your regeneration

- take as much time
as you need

once I had my heart
ripped right out
of my chest by someone
close to me

who knew exactly
what they were doing

and exactly how to
injure me

they were an expert on
exactly how to slice me

they turned their tongue
into a spear and said

"Your birth was a

John Roedel

a terrible mistake."

it was a sentence that ripped through me
it was a sentence that swallowed my light
it was a death sentence

I was instantly ruined

it almost left me dead

I had to be taken down
to this same river,

where it felt like I bled out every
single drop of blood inside of me

but the water never crimsoned
it remained unchanged

it stayed clear and translucent

at first, I fought the river,
I didn't believe I was worthy of it
I blamed myself for my trauma

but the flowing water
was so patient with
my retreating heart

- I sat in the stream of rippling healing
for at least a year before
I could find my feet again

so, take your time,
recovery doesn't own a watch

it will take exactly as long as
it needs to

you see,

healing

John Roedel

is a sacred
ritual
of resting

and of feasting
and of fasting
and of stillness
and of screaming
and of gardening
and of torching
and of falling
and of climbing
and of falling (again)
and of sewing
and of swearing
and of culling
and of crying
and of wandering
and of settling
and of rewriting
and of restlessness
and of surrendering
and of stitching
and of solitude
and of self-love
oh, and it's a ritual of forgiveness
(lots and lots of forgiveness)

it's a sacrament where water
becomes a divine seamstress
that stitches us back together

one teardrop at a time

- please, quit looking away
from the river

I know we just met

I know that I sound insane

I know none of this makes any sense

John Roedel

I know that your pain is telling you
not to trust me

I know you are suffering beyond anything
you could have ever imagined

I can feel your ache through my screen;
it's calling out to my ache like twins who
we're separated at birth

the thing is,

it only takes a single act of faith
to give redemption an opportunity
to make a home in us

so this is it

- this is your time
- this is your chance

take my hand and
come to the stream
take part in the
ritual of your recovery

stand among the flow

plant your bare feet in the mud
feel the great pull between
the gaps in your toes

that's your anointing
that's the blessing of remedy

can you feel it?

the moving reminder
that you were created
for more than this pain
you are enduring?

John Roedel

can you feel it?

the flowing hands of
unseen nurses tending
to your wounds?

can you feel Spirit rushing
around you - through you - in you?

that's the miracle of moving water
you've always known to be true

that's the current of rehabilitation
enveloping you - lapping at you with mercy

- now there is
just one more thing
you need the do before
the injury that you suffered
can be completely sealed

you have to say something
in order to remove any power
that your wound has over you

- and I'm not going to lie to you
saying this is going to hurt
a lot

but you have to say it if you
want the ritual to work

I'm sorry,
there is no other way

you will only have to say it once
and I will hold your hand while you do

I'll be right next to you the
whole time

John Roedel

- you are not alone - I am right here

to be mended you
must say the following
out loud:

"I am worthy of healing.
I don't deserve to suffer.
This is not my fault."

I understand how
hard those words
will be to utter

when I was in the river waiting to have
my heart put back in it took me an entire
month to form the words

it was agony

but the moment I said it
the ritual of recovery began
and the water to rose up to my chin

and the flow took away my pain
and my light started coming back to
me one celestial spark at a time

and I became the river;
I was all flow and no ebb

-I swear that the same thing will
happen for you

if you just take my hand
and say the words

"I am worthy of healing
- I don't deserve to suffer
- this is not my fault"

here we go

John Roedel

I'm right here

say it

"I am worthy of healing
- I don't deserve to suffer
- this is not my fault"

and you will start
be yourself once more

say it

"I am worthy of healing
- I don't deserve to suffer
- this is not my fault"

and your scars
will begin to vibrate

say it

"I am worthy of healing

-I don't deserve to suffer
- this is not my fault"

and you will be able
to stand again

I swear
my love,

you are worthy of healing
you do not deserve to suffer
this is not your fault

I swear

John Roedel

#13

be so very
careful

when trying to fit
in

with everybody
else

- because accidentally
someday

you just
might –

stay fully wild,
star child

ride your watermelon
bike

wear your purple polka dot
pants

dream your dripping honeycomb
dreams –

remain always untamed,
free spirit,

don't give up what makes you
different

be the red
umbrella

be the horseshoe
nebula

be the dancing

John Roedel

fool

be the mismatched
socks

be the walking piece of rainbow shag
carpet –

because

you weren't plucked from
nothingness

to simply fit
in

you were created to make us
gasp –

seduce us with your
strangeness

wear your authenticity like
lingerie

quit pretending to be so
khaki

while you are dripping in
watercolors –

continue being weird my
beautiful weirdo

- and remember remember remember

fitting in is for
sardines

John Roedel

#14

you'll know it's love
when you see it

if you have to
apologize for
being who you are

- it isn't love

if you have to
think about
it for too long

- it isn't love

if you have to
write a list of
pros and cons

- it isn't love

if you have to
worry about hiding
your scars

- it isn't love

if you have to
scrape a layer of ice
off your bedroom door

-it isn't love

if you have to
do some emotional algebra
to figure out if it's love

- it isn't love

love doesn't need
to be easy

John Roedel

but it should never
feel like you're in the mud

love is when they adore you
equally no matter if you are
wearing a sundress or
wearing nothing but rose petals or
wearing old pajamas

love is how you bite your
bottom lip unconsciously
when somebody says their name

love is how your skin
catches fire when they
walk into your room

love is how every time
that your hand fits inside
of theirs that you hear
the softest of clicks

love is a slow kiss
and a racing heart

if it's love
you'll know it
when you see it

it doesn't wear disguises
it doesn't pretend
it doesn't shape-shift

love is authentic

love can be born
from raw lust
and sometimes even loathing

but it should never return to
those wombs

John Roedel

and don't worry
if love hasn't arrived yet

- it will

love is likely taking
the scenic route

so it can pick
wildflowers
to give you on
your first date

while you are
waiting though

do me a favor
remind yourself of
something you knew long ago
that you have forgotten

you are worthy of love

you are
yes, you are

whisper it to yourself

"I am worthy of love"

trace it on your wrist
write it on the walls of your shower

you are worthy of love

and when it comes to you
you'll know it because of

how every one of your veins
will turn into Christmas lights

John Roedel

it will feel like an ancient truth

don't hide from love
stay on vigil

because it's coming to you
like a swarm of cherry blossoms
to wrap you up in scent and seduction
and safety and surrender

and when love finds you
to brush the hair out of
your eyes

you'll become weightless

that's how you'll know

- that it is love -

John Roedel

#15

Don't ever apologize
for how you heal.

John Roedel

#16

there's no handbook
for any of this

there are no hard and
fast rules for times
like these

you're doing the best you can

holding things together
while the world falls apart

in this age of fear and fret
you don't need to be perfect;
you just need to be gentle

with yourself and everyone else
because that's all you
can really control, isn't it?

yes, things might unravel a
bit more before this is
all done

you might as well

and it's okay if
you do

while the world
is resetting
it's router

we can take turns
deciding who gets
to cry on the couch

we can take turns becoming
a balm for one another

John Roedel

we can take turns yelling
up into the silent sky

we can take turns
having insomnia

we can take turns being
confessionals for one another

we can take turns brushing
the tears off of each other's face

don't worry about getting
all of this right

you won't

don't worry about making
mistakes

you will

- you're doing the best you can

there is only one great commandment for
enduring a storm - and it's this:

go easy,
my love,
go easy

John Roedel

#17

untying the invisible knots
around your wrist and getting
out of bed in the morning
to feed your children breakfast

is courage

gazing into the mirror and
looking past the new wrinkles
time brushed on you while you slept
and reminding yourself of your
natural elegance

is also courage

walking out the front door of your
house even though there is a
red ghost on your porch shrieking
"They'll never understand you!

is also courage

dropping your children off at school
and reminding them of their royalty
despite the dented car they are getting
out of and the faded box store jeans
they are wearing

is also courage

singing along to the song playing on your
car's radio that you used to belt out at the
tops of your lungs with your best friend
who stopped calling you a couple of years ago
because you aren't "fun anymore"

is also courage

smiling your way through another one of

John Roedel

your perfect coworker's stories about how
difficult their perfect body, perfect children
perfect credit score and perfect sex life is while
not breaking down into tears

is also courage

sitting alone at lunch with just a plastic fork
digging its way through week-old leftovers
and silently going over in your mind which bills
you can afford to skip out on paying this month

is also courage

checking Instagram and "liking" the
photos your sister posted from her
family's most recent vacation to some
small island that you've never heard of

is also courage

brushing the tears from your child's
face who had their heart broken at
school and telling her that it will be better
tomorrow when that has yet to be your
experience

is also courage

sleeplessly laying in your bed at night
watching your ceiling fan lumber and
despite the hole in your heart you quietly
offer a simple prayer of thanksgiving
to God for your life

is also courage

my love,

you are the living
gospel of courage

John Roedel

every passage of your story that you write
earns you another unseen
medal of valor

you are bravery in motion
you are the picture of courageousness

nothing you do is ordinary
- everything you do is heroic
    - every little bit of it

going grocery shopping on a budget takes courage
checking your bank account takes courage
brushing your thinning hair takes courage
not slapping stupid people takes courage
taking a compliment takes courage
dreaming about being kissed again takes courage
doing a single load of laundry takes courage
texting your mom takes courage
looking through old pictures takes courage
screaming into a pillow in the middle of the night takes courage
letting yourself laugh takes courage
sitting in a church pew takes courage
clinging onto an ounce of hope takes courage
sitting through well-intended advice from a friend takes courage

it's all part of your living gospel of courage

holding your phone in your shaking hand
brushing your fingers over the screen
typing in a phone number
that you can't remember when it was
the last time that you called it

- because of their pride
and because of your pride

and because of the scars you gave each other
and because sometimes life gets away
from us like a salmon in a river

and then the phone rings in your flushed ear,

John Roedel

and then your breath becomes hot,
and then you wait to hear their voice again,
and then you wait to hear them
finally, say "I've missed you."
and then you both cry,
and then you hear yourself,
finally, say out loud for the first time in years

"I need help...."

that is also courage
that is also courage
that is also courage

don't give up
oh, my love,
do t give up

- you are the living gospel of courage
    that I can't wait to read from cover to cover

John Roedel

#18

remaining delicate
doesn't make you weak

it makes you willing to get
shattered every now and then

in order for you to transform
into whatever
you need to become next

some of God's best
artwork

are things that were
once broken

that became a new creation

if someday you
have to become
completely undone

- don't fight it

because that is just a sign
that the divine isn't done
working on you yet

if someday the forest
of your life has to
be burned to the ground

-don't cling to the ashes of what once was

just stand still and wait
patiently for the
saplings of what comes
next for you

- **emerge emerge emerge**

John Roedel

being willing to
start over
again and again
is the opposite
of weakness

it's the toughest
thing I can think of

resurrection is only
for the strong

and you, my love,

you are the strongest
person I have
ever met

John Roedel

#19

I know how
difficult this
life can be

the journey
is often so
hard, Isn't it?

and I know
what it is
like

having a brain
that is constantly
bickering with
your heart

while the three
of you try and
climb up an ever
steepening mountain

I know you
want to quit

to just let go
of the stone
wall and to

fall
fall
fall

but I also
know that
right now

there is a
voice inside of
you saying

John Roedel

"Hold on
just one
more day.

I love you.

You are
going to
make it.

You are
star fire
that will
burn long
after this
moment.

You are
a sing bird
whose song
has an endless
refrain.

"I love you."

You can call this
voice whatever
you want

your conscience
your soul
your God
your angel
your ego
your ancestors
your spirit

it doesn't
matter to me
what you
call this voice

John Roedel

or where that
you think it

comes from
I only care
that you listen
to it

the voice inside
of you that is
begging you
to keep going
is like an unseen
conch shell
that is being held
up to your ears
with invisible hands

my love,
listen to
the voice

I know that
you know it's there

I know you've
heard it speak to you before

listen to what
it's saying to you

your story doesn't
end with you
giving up

you are the ripple
that still has a
long way to go

I know how it
feels to be Invisibly

John Roedel

wounded

and to be forced
to smile and
shake hands as

if you aren't
bleeding out

I know
I know
I know

what it feels like
to want to loosen
your grip on the
mountain and fall

but you
can't

because that
voice inside of
you is still talking
to you

listen to it

how will you
know that
you're listening
to the right voice?

because it will sound
exactly like yours –

I know how much
you are struggling
right now

I can feel your
ache in my bones

John Roedel

look away from
the screen

take a deep
breath

put your hand
on your heart

close your eyes

and listen to
the voice inside
of you recite

the lyrics of
how you
will survive

listen to the
unseen conch shell
breathing hope
in your ears

"I love you.

You are
going to
make it.

You are
the star fire
that will keep
burning long
after your
pain goes away.

You are
a sing bird
whose song
has an endless

John Roedel

refrain.

"I love you."

John Roedel

#20

oh, my love,

I know you've been wounded
- and I know you feel incomplete

you don't owe anybody an explanation
for how you were hurt

you don't owe us anything other than the
promise you'll keep playing your hymn

you didn't know you were a hymn?

oh, my love,

you're the loveliest madrigal
I have ever heard

the holes in your heart don't
make you broken

the holes in your heart make
you an instrument of holy wind

passing the great howl
softly through you

- I can hear your melody
soothing me from miles away

you turn blustering storms into an overture
and gales into dawdling chords

you are a lighthouse of siren serenades
inviting me into the safe harbor or your touch

in a world that demands completeness

I am seduced with
how perfectly unfinished you are

John Roedel

the pieces you are missing in your heart
play the most wonderful notes

- at night I long to place
my back against yours

so I can syncopate to the timbre of your soul

I can feel the heat and drumbeat of your song
thumping against my thin skin

can I lay unencumbered in
your arms for a bit longer

until I drift to sleep under
the harmony of your scars?

every little thing that has broken off of you
has transformed you into a symphony

the holes the world have put in
your heart are the gaps that have
made you a woodwind
instrument of the great spirit

you are a clarinet of courage
you are a flute of felicity
you are an oboe of originality
you are the bassoon of beauty

the universe is finally done holding its breath
and has turned your wounds into an embouchure

taking every cut that you've endured
and passing its divine breath through you

so the rest of us can sit under a sky full of
stars and listen to the concert of your grace

oh my love, can't you
see it now?

John Roedel

the places you've been hurt
and the holes in your
heart you've received

emit the soundtrack
of your untamed heart

everything that you've overcome
plays a score that leaves
me so overcome by you

oh, my love, you are the hymn
that I could listen to all-day

John Roedel

#21

the words we form
on our tongues

can become bombs
or acorns

every time we speak
to each other
we have the choice

to ruin

or to raise
each other

when I die
will I be surrounded
by a forest of comforting
words that I planted?

or will my final
resting place be
an ashpit where I
detonated my pride
over and over?

oh, Spirit

help me grow
a grove of
kindness that
stretches from
valley to valley

oh, Divine Light,

help me become
an arborist of hope
whose redwoods

John Roedel

hold treehouse chapels
where the congregants
hold hands and count
each other's tears

oh, Mysterious Love,

help me cultivate
a vast wilderness of
empathy and mercy
whose soft bark smells
like mountain lilies and
where the blooms yawn
themselves awake while
singing cosmic psalms

oh, Unending Creator,

help me become a courageous
Johnny Appleseed that refuses to
cut down trees to build an
ark out of my self-righteousness
where I can float away on
the suffering of this world

oh, Mystical Mover of My Heart,

teach me how to let every word
I utter be a source of shade
instead of a cause for shame

before I return the source

I want to plant
roots of love so
deep into this world

that they get tangled
up in the mantle

and keeps the
world from spinning

John Roedel

quite as madly as it
does today

this is my purpose

to turn my acorns into action
to turn goodwill into a Giant Sequoia
to turn branches into bright pew bench
to turn judgment into a jungle of kindness

this is why I'm here
and not to sound too preachy
- but I think it's why you are here too

we are here to grow
the most incredible towering
trees of compassion
for each other to climb in

oh, Eternal Artist

help us replace our nooses
with tire swings

so we can take turns rocking
back and forth under the thickets
of our most gentle wishes for
each other

back and forth
back and forth
back and forth

John Roedel

#22

"read this in case the light takes me first"

* * * * *

it appears that I fell out of my body
-and right up into the light
and no, it doesn't really bother me
-that I've lost all of my sight

because now I can see with
-the wide eyes of my heart
and I can no longer tell
-my friends or foes apart

currently, I'm out deep in space
-watching the birth of a baby star
yet despite our physical separation
-from you, my soul's never that far

tomorrow, I'll be picking flowers
-in the garden out near the edge of time
I can send you a rose by angel mail
-if of my survival, you need a fragrant sign

my love, I know you'll come to find me
-once you'll fall up into the light, too
and we'll slow dance by disco nebulas
-and kiss until purple comets blush blue

our reunion will be an interstellar romantic ritual
-out here among the burst of creation's first light
where the two of us will become an Andromeda knot
-that is tied together so softly -yet tangled so tight

and when our souls become one
-we'll open up our own little cosmic shop
we'll call our boutique "Death Isn't Real"
-since the love between us never stopped

tethered as one we will spend ten billion years

John Roedel

-until the bolts of eternity start to unscrew
yet I won't fear the great resetting of time
-because it means I'll get to discover you anew

so, my love, when forever starts all over
-we'll both fall back into our new skin
and we'll find each other on an alien shore
-to let our love story start all over again

John Roedel

#23

my love,

I can see by the exact way you
are holding the tears back
and by how your bottom lip
trembles every time I ask you
if you're okay

that

you are planning
on giving up
on your life today

- I'm sorry, but it turns out
that you just don't
have the time to die today

- instead

you're going to be
too busy with

counting all of the people
who will miss you
if you leave this
world before it's
your time to go

and then counting
all of the people
you haven't met
yet that are going
to need you to
tell them your
story of how you
survived this terrible
moment in time

then after that you

John Roedel

are scheduled for

chasing down
all of the
little miracles and
wonders that the
angels left for
you outside
of your house

{hint: these miracles and wonders
are usually near gardens, moving water,
starlit skies or dangling from
the branches of nearby trees}

and once you're done with all of that
your time will be occupied with

breathing in and out
with such a deep
intention that

the air in your lungs will
become a sacred prayer and
your veins fill up with
rushing mercy

and then you'll have to
speed over to your next
planned event which is:

laying your head
in the lap of a
beloved as you
pour out the contents
on your broken heart
one honest teardrop
at a time

and before you go
to bed tonight you
 are already booked

John Roedel

for

spending time
with your inner child
who will hold your
hand and whisper
a secret to you
that it appears that
you have long forgotten

"All storms pass."
and then after that
you have a standing
date with God

who plans on
swaddle you
while you sleep

to the metronome
of your peaceful
newborn heart

can't you see?

you are way too busy
to give up on yourself
today

by the way,
before you ask

I already checked
your schedule for
tomorrow

and it's even
busier

I'm sorry,
it appears

John Roedel

that you can't
give into
your despair
any time soon

you have
way too much
to do

you just won't any have
free moments to
spend it leaving us

turns out that
holding on to hope
is a full-time job

and you have
so much more
work ahead of you

John Roedel

#24

different isn't another word for broken
different is beautiful

when tempted to try and "fix" someone
who does not live their life as you do

let them be
please let them be

we aren't here to domesticate wildflowers
we are here to learn to become one ourselves

different isn't another word for broken
different is beautiful

John Roedel

#25

you found me
sobbing on
the lawn

and you asked
me why I was crying

I forced a smile and said
"my heart keeps breaking"

I expected you to
try and talk me out
of my breakdown

instead you
simply touched
my wet face with
your open palm

and my tears
sunk into your
soft skin

like a seeds

and suddenly
a small vine
with pink blooms
grew out of your wrist

and it wrapped
around me

and suddenly there
were dozens of
these little vines with
these pink blooms

sprouting out of
you and swaddling

John Roedel

themselves all over me

and suddenly the space
that once existed between us
became a garden of pastel
mercy

and suddenly I heard a
thunderclap inside of me

suddenly every single tear
I was hoarding started
to downpour out of my eyes
down into the soil
of your kindness

and suddenly you began
to glow like a blazing sun
and the garden we were
growing became thick
and wild

suddenly I could
only smell the flowering
fragrance of peace

- that, to me,
smelled just like lilacs,
though I'm told it smells
differently for everyone –

and suddenly I could feel
one of your vines slip in
under one of my scars
and wrap around my heart

and suddenly
I could feel the vine
stitching my broken pieces
back together

and suddenly the other vines

John Roedel

lifted us both off of the ground
and up into the late August sky

and suddenly we became
tangled up together in the
sky jungle paradise
of connection that can only exist
between two trembling humans

oh, my love,
there are so many miracles
that can happen when
a tear dropper meets
a tear catcher

it causes a chemical reaction
that makes every other element
to gawk and gather

it causes a cosmic reaction
that summons an angel
to come and sing us love songs
from the trees

oh, empathy,
is my favorite form
of magic

sometimes the simplest
of questions can
grow a new Eden

sometimes the simplest
of acts of mercy can
restart Genesis

oh, my love,
thank you for asking
what was wrong

John Roedel

#26

Recently, as I was sitting in an Arby's drive-thru line I unexpectedly began to sob.

I'm talking about the level of sobbing that had anybody noticed me I might have had been admitted for observation in a nearby mental health institution for 48 hours.

Like most of my emotional breaks, it came out of the blue - but this one felt like much more of a downpour than any teardrop cloudburst I had recently experienced.

It was an earthquake taking place in the very mantle of my soul. The emotional explosion inside of me was so deep that I could feel new fault lines form.

I felt every fiber of my core shaking and swaying. The caverns inside of me were collapsing. The mineshafts I use to mine for gold in my heart were being buried under my trembling form. Suddenly, I was in the middle of a full-on emotional implosion that arrived without an announcement or invitation.

I really cannot remember what it was that triggered me into this specific breakdown. I have been living on the edge of my emotions lately so it could have really been anything.

Maybe the anxieties that usually wait for me under my bed at night decided to show up at lunchtime just to prove they aren't always daysleepers.

Maybe it was the sappy bumper sticker of a car in front of me? It was the one that featured a stick figure family holding hands. Those stickers always make me nostalgic for a time in my life when my kids were little and enjoyed tangling their little fingers in mine. I so miss the warmth of their racing pulses beating against my own.

Maybe it was the song that had been playing on the radio at the time? It was a lovely song that had a bunch of piano and violin woven in it. Perhaps the beauty of that instrumental combination

John Roedel

ripped a hole in my onion paper composure that I attempt to walk around with?

I really have no clue what reduced me into a blubbering cliche of faucet eyes and dry heaves - but whatever it was - it got me good. What I did know was that I had to pull myself together quickly.

There were only three cars in front of me before I got to the window to pick up my food. I didn't want the teenager handing me my Beef N' Cheddar to feel compelled to ask me if I was alright.

In my writing life I wear my heart on my sleeve - but in my life outside of the page, I try to keep my emotions kenneled like it was a puppy with a leaky bladder.

However, as it turns out, while in the midst of a full-on meltdown there is no trickier feat to pull off than to try and calm down quickly.

I kept sucking in deep breaths as I had just been pulled out of a riptide - but with every inhalation I took in my breathing became more and more jagged.

The more I rubbed my eyes the more tears it produced. They were acting like lemons that were being squeezed of my humanity that was now streaming all over my face.

Arby's drive-thrus are normally a stop-motion experience in customer service. You can spend an entire week waiting for an overpriced mountain of slow-roasted goodness - but not on this day.

On this particular day, the fine people operating this particular franchise had their act together.

The drive-thru line was moving quickly and by the time it was my turn at the window I was in full melancholy bloom.

I rolled down my window and the teenager (whom I am guessing was not a trained mental health professional) came face-to-face with a middle-aged man in a full-on emotional crisis.

John Roedel

She handed me my unsweet tea with a look on her face that indicated her Arby's handbook had never quite prepared her for this kind of moment with a customer.

She was really quite lovely about the whole encounter. I have blocked a lot of it out of my memory (due to the toxic levels of cringe-worthy things I think I said to her) but here is a brief snippet of how our interaction went:

Fast Food Teenager: Sir, are you okay?

Me: Who knows...

Fast Food Teenager: Um. Can I do anything to help?

Me: Can I have a couple of extra packets of horsey sauce?

On the way home to finish eating my feelings, I admonished myself over and over for my inability to keep myself together in public.

I was ashamed of my outburst. An outburst that I still couldn't put my finger on where it had actually come from.

I was raised to treat my emotions like a secret garden that can only be accessed during blue moons in April. What I had just done was blasphemy for how my parents instructed me to operate.

However, by the time I pulled up in front of my house I had come to a different revelation.

I think part of the reason why I am exhausted all of the time is that I'm spending so much effort burying my feelings under a couple of miles of prideful granite.

What is the harm in letting other people know that I am just as human as they are?

There is none.

John Roedel

In fact, I have convinced myself that the teenage fast-food worker who had caught a glimpse of my breakdown was given permission to show her feelings to the world more authentically.

Perhaps that wasn't her takeaway from our encounter and perhaps the story of her interaction with a weepy penguin-looking man is now being passed around Snapchat - but that's okay too.

I am done apologizing for being human.

As I sat in my driveway consuming my lukewarm roast beef sandwich I wrote the following poem about how I plan to quit hiding my wounds from the world.

I knew that if I didn't write about it at that moment that I would forget exactly how I felt.

Yes, I had made myself into a spectacle but at least I got a poem and a couple of extra packets of horsey sauce out of it.

With eyes stinging and my nose running I wrote the following poem:

If you haven't had a
complete breakdown
in public

I highly recommend it

- it's like being an ice cream
cone sitting upright on
a summer sidewalk

where you feel exactly like
a skeleton of fragile wafer
bones trying to keep all of
our your sweet sadness inside
of you from spilling out on
the warm pavement

causing your neighbor
to walk over you

John Roedel

on her way to
take her daughter to her
modern dance class

"Look out for that mess, honey,"
the mom will say as
she guides her child past the puddle
that you are forming into

"Don't get any of that on your shoes."
the little girl will look at you
and you will look at her

- a moment of connection between
the two of you

before her mom lightly will pinch her
arm to get her to quit staring at you

- but it will be too late

you will have given the little girl
permission to act human in public

my love,

you need to know that
in that moment of your public breakdown
you won't feel any shame

I know you think that you will
but you won't

you will feel something else

- authenticity

like you aren't living your life
for other people anymore

like you finally living
for yourself

John Roedel

I know it's a cliche for
me to say that it sometimes
takes losing your mind
to find your voice

but it's true

the more we melt
outside of the cage
we put ourselves in

the more we become
what we are meant to be:

- a human with
changing seasons

does the thunderhead feel self-conscious
when it booms above a valley?

does the snow care if it covers a rooftop
under a blanket of fresh powder?

does the sun race to hide behind the moon
whenever people witness it dance in the sky?

does the rain fret about what we will think
about it as it cries all over our flowers?

no, they don't

the seasons just be
the season they need to be
- and they do so unafraid

and you should just
be who you need to be
- and you should do so unafraid

don't bury your flame under the soil
don't hide your tears beneath sunglasses

John Roedel

don't use your hand to cover your smile
don't put your song on the lowest volume

if God wanted us to conceal our emotions
we would have been born with yarn sewn
on us for lips and buttons stitched in for eyes

we'd be expressionless puppets
we'd be static zombies
we'd be easy to forget

our emotions are what gives us power
our emotions are what tie us to the divine
our emotions are what melody behind our lyrics

be real

if you feel like glowing - light the room up with your shine

if you have to blizzard - cover the valley in your ice

if you have to rain - saturate the ground until sunflowers bloom

if you have to thunder - break my eardrums

we have been told for years
to keep it all in

because if we let people see that we care
about how brutal and lovely this experience
of being alive really is that it may cause them to think less of us

if that's the case then I want the world
to have the lowest opinion of me possible

I want the world to see me as a tangle of cords
I want the world to see me as an unmade bed
I want the world to see me as a volatile season
I want the world to see me as a puddle of ice cream

I want the world to know me as a human

John Roedel

don't keep it all in
let your seasons out

and if you need to break down
in public

go right ahead

cry without shame

trace your fingers on your scars
sing your sorrow

because when you do
a little kid might see you

and feel like they can be themselves too
and to finally have permission to finally

live authentically too

John Roedel

#27

"I feel like I'm running out of time to experience all that I want to in life."

"What is it that you want to do with the time you have left?

"Only the most important things."

"Okay, you should get started. What's on the top of your list that you really want to do?"

"To just sit here with you and count the freckles around your eyes"

"I thought you only wanted to do important things?"

"And that's exactly what I'm doing."

***

if you let anything
be an adventure

then everything can be
an adventure

or is it the other around?

no matter, my love
please listen, this is important

even the most routine moment
can become a once-in-a-lifetime marvel

if you honor the ludicrous wonderment of
your very existence

I know we just met but I have
a very personal question to ask you

how do you think you

John Roedel

got here on Earth?

do you believe that you
are you a cosmic accident
that came from a bunch of
stars crashing into each other
for a couple of billion years?

if so, what a miracle you are!

you won the universal power ball
you are the most valuable scratch ticket ever
you are the culmination of a trillion coincidences
you became you despite the vast nothingness

there is nothing ordinary about you

and whether you know it or not

your life is the rose in the desert
your life is the book that can't be burned
your life is the campfire in the wastelands
your life is the thing that keeps death up at night

you are a miracle

or maybe
you believe that you
are a creation of the divine
who spent so much time
and love sculpting you into
the work of art you are now?

if so, what a miracle you are!

you have been plucked out of nothingness
you are the result of a carefully created blueprint
you were kissed in the womb by visiting angels
you are the living witness of an everlasting love

there is nothing ordinary about you

John Roedel

and whether you know it or not

your life is the rose in the desert
your life is the book that can't be burned
your life is the campfire in the wasteland
your life is the thing that keeps death up at night

you are a miracle

my love,

regardless of where we came from
the fact that our hearts and brains
and lungs and eyes and knees and
spines and skin and lips and fingernails
and cells and veins and taste buds and
everything else that was somehow gifted to

us

all work together in such a delicate
balance to keep our adventure
going is all the proof that there is
no such thing as a boring moment

being bored is just code for I already
understand the mystery of life and
it no longer excites me

being bored is an excuse we give ourselves
for not appreciating the absolute bonkers
the phenomenon that is taking place every single
time we do anything as simple as itch our nose

our brain sends a signal
to our finger to move

and just like
magic suddenly
our finger
is scratching
our nose

John Roedel

that sounds like a miracle to me
that sounds like magic to me
that sound like science fiction to me

I have so much to do in life
that it drives me mad

I want to tell jokes to audiences soaked in wine
I want to write a poem that is read at a funeral
I want to eat a meal on a Hawaiian beach at sunset
I want to not worry about money anymore
I want to sing a song outside your window
I want to learn to speak Italian
I want to visit every corner of our world
I want to have coffee with God just once
I want to watch the whales migrate
I want to paint a big fat tree
I want to parachute over a jungle
I want to finally finish something I start
I want to teach my kids how to fish
I want to find peace
I want to ride in a spaceship
I want to jump into a perfect reflection in the water

I have so much that I want to do
but I can't do any of it

because I'm stuck in the sticky taffy
lie that we all get tangled up in

-it's the lie that life
can be ordinary and boring

- but it isn't
not one second of it is

it's all a miracle

all
of
it

John Roedel

even when we aren't doing anything
but sitting on the couch together
counting each other's freckles

we are doing something amazing

we are embracing the grand spectacle
of our ridiculous novel existence

- we just don't recognize it yet

my love,

if I accomplish anything in my life
let it be this

let me finally appreciate
the splendor of our portent, jim-dandy,
crackerjack, fleeting, flashing,
corker adventure that every single
moment of being alive offers me

even if I'm doing nothing
it's all so very everything

John Roedel

#28

I'm so sorry to wake you up
but there is something
that I have to tell you
before the dawn arrives

I need you to believe something

-the sadness that lays
heavy on your chest like a
century-old cannonball
isn't who you are

-the ghost that lives
in your inner ear and
lies to you about your beauty
isn't who you are

-the swarm of regret wasps
that have turned your
heart into a dripping hive of guilt

isn't who you are

-the burning itch under your
sweet skin that begs for you to
tear into so you'll finally feel something
isn't who you are

-the thick knot in your
stomach that has been
there since your first memory
isn't who you are

oh, my love,

you aren't any of
the terrors

that have made a home
inside of you

John Roedel

they are squatters
who believe that
just because they
left their dirty socks
under your bed that
they have a say in
who you are

they don't

can I finally tell you
the truth of why
you were created?

- well, I'm going to anyway

the truth is
you were created
to be the moonlight on
an unmoving lake

reflecting the mystery
of our never-ending universe
in your eyes

I swear I can
see a nebula
just inside of
left your pupil

you are the burning
fire in the sky

you are moonlight on the water

and by simply being alive
you are silently inviting the

rest of us to sit by your
shore so that we can bathe
our scars in the shimmer of

John Roedel

your sweet celestial smile

- you. are. moonlight. on. the. water.

that's why you were created
    - I promise

don't believe the interlopers

you are the delicate light
of heaven's eternal gaze

do you believe that yet?

I know you don't see it yet
 - but you will

you have let these
devils live inside of
you for too long

you've become
used to them

- but it's time for them to go

the moonlight on the water
doesn't need to be obscured

you shine best when the clouds
are invited to leave

we need you to be
at your brightest

I know it sounds selfish
but I need your light

I know it sounds selfish
but I need your light
to keep me alive

John Roedel

for both of us,
it's time to let all of
the interlopers go
   - every single one of them

-the cannonball
      -the ghost
         -the wasp
            -the burning itch
                  -the thick knot

it's time for them to go

open the door
unzip the tent
break the windows
unlock the gate
bulldoze the fence

I don't care how you do it
but don't let them stay inside
of you anymore

those things aren't who you are,
remember?

you are the moonlight
on the water

remember?

everything you want
is waiting for you
on the other side
of what you are currently
suffering through

you aren't what is
happening to you

you aren't the pain
you aren't the anxiety

John Roedel

you aren't the regret

you are the moonlight on the water

oh, my love,
the horizon is yawning
here comes the new day

do you believe me, yet?

John Roedel

#29

-I know how they hurt you

I know how they
squeezed your
heart and throat until
you couldn't love
or breathe easy

I'm so sorry that happened

-I know how they hurt you

I know how they
screamed at you
until the rose inside
of you wilted under
their hot September fury

I'm so sorry that happened

-I know how they hurt you

I know how they
mocked you
whenever you told
them what
your dreams were

I'm so sorry that happened

-I know how they hurt you

I know how they
tied you to a chair just
so they could explain
to you why they believe
that you aren't
equal to them

I'm so sorry that happened

John Roedel

-I know how they hurt you

I know how they filled
your pockets with rocks
and threw you in the
river to see if you could
somehow float

I'm so sorry that happened

-I know how they hurt you

I know how they turned
their religion into a
whip so that could leave
a scar on your back that
looks like a dove

I'm so sorry that happened

-I know how they hurt you

I know how they looked
at you as an object they
owned and had no
problem reminding you
about that every day

I'm so sorry that happened

-I know how they hurt you

I know how they cursed
you with the terror of
self-doubt, self-loathing,
self-pity self-destruction
and self-harm

I'm so sorry that happened

-I know how they hurt you

John Roedel

I know how they made you
to feel ugly by replacing
all of the mirrors in your
home with photos of you
during your very worst moments

I'm so sorry that happened

-I know how they hurt you

I know how they
bruised you so often
and so deeply that
eventually your body
began to look like lent

I'm so sorry that happened

-I know how they hurt you

I know how they never
let you think or vote for
or believe in anything
other than what they
told you to

I'm so sorry that happened

-I know how they hurt you

I know how they turned
your bedroom into a
dark alley with the only
way of it would be to
wait for the tardy dawn

I'm so sorry that happened

-I know how they hurt you

I know how they broke you on

John Roedel

the inside and then complained
about how noisy the shattered
pieces in you were whenever
you walked around

I'm so sorry that happened

But

they can't touch you
any more

you are safe
now

here in this garden
with me

you are
protected

take off your
armor

let the sunlight kiss
your soft skin

take off your
armor

you won't need
it today

take off your
armor

you can walk
easy and unencumbered

take off your
armor

John Roedel

don't let the bastards
win by making you
hide under hot metal plates

the wounds they gave
you won't be telling the
story of how protective
you became

your wounds are telling
the story of how you
kept going long after
they tried to kill you

your wounds are telling
the story of how they
tried to burn you into
ashes but couldn't

take off your
armor

tell me your beautiful story
of how you became the

-untouchable
-unscratchable
-undying

diamond in the sky

take off your
armor

and

-sit with me in
this garden

until you remember
who you were
before they hurt you

John Roedel

until you trust in
being vulnerable again

-sit with me in
this garden

until you
are yourself
again

-sit with me in
this garden

until you
believe you
are worthy
of being healed

-sit with me in
this garden

until we are
covered in
the fragrant
marigolds

of your coming recovery

John Roedel

#30

God didn't use
a calculator or
a tape measure
while creating

you

the Divine didn't follow
a technical manual
when connecting
the wires in your

heart

the Great Mystery didn't
use a beaker to brew your
soul before carefully
pouring it into your

body

creation didn't sketch out
your design out a couple
of times before starting to
shape you from the cosmic

clay

spirit wasn't concerned
with how things have
been done before while
imagining you into

existence

the studio where you were created
remains covered in the wildest colors
of spilled paint

there is still a strand of glitter stuck up

John Roedel

on the ceiling where Eternity first breathed
life into your lungs

God made the most beautiful
mess while making you

you are a Monet in blue jeans

and you weren't created
to be symmetrically
perfect

you were created
to be a lopsided vessel
of raw uncut beauty

you weren't created
with sharp angles

you were created
surrounded by angels

the very first spark
of you was taken
from the wildfire
of the Divine's
burning love

you are a wonderful
experiment of grace and
miracle that has
changed the world

by just being

the Master Artist
created you both

thoughtfully
and without any restraint

because that

John Roedel

are what all
masterpieces need

all timeless
works of art
need equal
measures of

- careful precision
- and untamed passion

and you, my love
are as timeless
as any artwork
that has existed

God is still
covered in
the same glue
that was used
to keep you
from falling apart

so, my love,

whenever you are sitting
with your feet dangling
over the edge of your
darkest thoughts

and you are tempted
to just lean over the
cliff and fall into
the oblivion of despair

remember that
every particle in
you has been kissed
by a Creator who
stitched you together
with the loveliest
sequins, feathers, and flowers

John Roedel

that could be found
on the most remote
reaches of the universe

remember you
have been embroidered
in purpose

remember you
are splashed
with pastel colored
stardust that makes
your neckline
glow like galaxy
fireflies when the sun
goes down

remember that you
are a living work
of art unlike any that has
ever been seen before

quit worrying about your
imperfections

those are your
watercolors
that bled over
each other
on that canvas
of your life

even sunsets
can't keep
from coloring
outside of the lines

so why should you?

you were made out
of the most chaotic
and beautiful of messes

John Roedel

by an Artist who wanted
to show the universe what
true beauty looks like

you are the Magnum-Opus
of God's wild love

you are a living treasure
that was never meant to
be hidden behind a glass case
or a velvet rope

you are the covered
in the brushstrokes of
fire and dreams

you are a singular
portrait of holy wonder

so,
you better
start treating yourself like it

John Roedel

#31

when the world
goes mad

be wildly kind
to everyone

everyone
everyone
everyone

- you can't control
much

but you control how
you treat others

in these breaking news
heartbreaking times

when nothing feels
certain

let your raw kindness
be a certainty

allow your compassion
to become a North Star

stamped up in
the sky for

others to follow
back home

John Roedel

#32

oh, my love,
I could see that you were
deep in thought

- but I couldn't help myself
from interrupting you

I'm sorry for being rude – but

I had a question for you
that I was unable to shake

my curiosity had sprouted as a sapling
and then grew into a redwood with more
branches than I could ever count

I couldn't escape it

- the question tied had
itself to my tongue

- I had to ask you

I drew a cautious breath
and approached the
altar of your amber eyes

"My love?" I asked

you looked up at me through
the billowing steam rising up
from your peppermint tea

spilling your smile open like an ark
that held a hundred million graces

My love," I repeated. "Why have you
been so quiet lately?"

your smile didn't fade,

John Roedel

- if anything it widened

- like you had been waiting
for me to finally have
the courage to ask my question

you reached across the
kitchen table

and laid your hand on mine
as if it were a picnic blanket

softly, you said to me:

"Because I'm healing,"

your hand squeezed mine
and suddenly I couldn't
find my voice to offer
a follow-up question

for the first time in my life
I was mute

suddenly it all made sense

wounds are so loud

- injuries are like roars
- being hurt always makes such a clamor
- getting damaged is often so deafening

but the act of restoration
is so very silent

it's a rose petal falling
on a cotton bed

the murmur of healing
is just like that
of a sleeping newborn

John Roedel

humming calmly
in the arms of their mother

the repair of our
soul takes place
under a canopy of
divine lullabies

recovery often
arrives in a hush

- like vespers being
delicately sung
at sunrise in a stone
monastery

the voice of renewal
gently echoes off
the walls

inviting us to fall into the near
noiseless sound of our punctured
heart being filled with hope once again

calling us to sit in stillness as
all the rips we have torn in
each other are being sewn back
together by the seamstress
of forgiveness

my love,
your silence has taught me that

being made whole again is
usually an inaudible miracle

healing doesn't bang a gong
or ring a bell

in fact, the only sound healing makes
is one of a babbling brook in the distance

John Roedel

- calling us follow it

and to discover the
moving water that
will make us new

if we just lay down
in its holy flow

- oh, my love, my scars are
always ringing in my ears

and it always sounds like the echo of my
past injuries screaming at me from the past

- my love, can you teach me
your secrets of inaudible healing?

-teach me how to be so very quiet
-teach me how to be so very still
-teach me how to be so very humble

while I'm being made whole again

and my love, teach me how
to listen so very carefully

to the wonderful
silence of
my coming recovery

John Roedel

#33

I woke up
this morning
afraid that I had
begun my last day

so

I tightened the
faucets on all of
the clocks in my house

until every minute
felt like it was a fat
droplet of water
resting on the lip
of a spigot

that it clung to

just before letting go
and splashing on
my bare toes

and now time is
just dripping by me
in slow motion

my love,

I have discovered
how less scary the world
is when it isn't
pouring through my
fingers all at once

- when I take life
just one easy
drop at a time

things don't feel

John Roedel

so overwhelming

and I'm
starting to
stare at each
leisurely forming
bead of time

like the unhurried
marvel it is

like the unique
little bulb of
reflected light

it was made to be

and now
I think I
might just
make it
another day

my love,

-when this life
isn't a rushing flood
of blurred moments

it's so damn
beautiful

-when life becomes
a deliberate pitter-patter
of wonderment

it's all exactly
what I imagined
it was going
to be like before
I was born

John Roedel

Remedy 123

it's a downpour of
life that comes down
one methodical
dripp-ity drop
of time at a time

drop
I can make it

drop
I can make it

drop
it's all a miracle

drop
it's all such an adventure

drop
I can't wait to see what comes next

drop
thank you, Creation for giving me another day

drop
I can make it

drop
I can make it

drop
oh, my love,

drop
I'm not scared anymore

drop
I can see angels in the clouds now

drop
I think I am going to be okay

John Roedel

drop
I can make it

oh, my love, I can make it
dropdropdropdropdrop

John Roedel

#34

Is it your turn to forgive me
or
is it my turn to forgive you?

I can't remember either.

To be safe we better just forgive
each other at the exact same time.

Here's how:

We will hold hands
so that your wrist
presses right up
against mine.

And now we wait
until our pulses
match each other.

And now we close our
eyes and pretend
that our veins are
rivers of empathy

and now the seasons are changing

and now the mountains are melting
and now the water is rising
and now the rivers are growing together

and now the barren
space we let grow
between us is being
flooded with stretching
vineyards of clemency

and now exotic wildflowers
are growing everywhere

John Roedel

everywhere
everywhere
everywhere

and now all we know is an ocean

and now we are swimming
in the same tides of understanding

and now the two of us are endless again

and now we are the
newborn children of forgiveness

open your eyes
look down at our wrists
wrapped around each other

and now I forgive you
and now you forgive me

and now I see you
and now you see me

and now can't you feel it?

- this rising river
- this rolling ocean
- this endless us

this rushing mercy

John Roedel

#35

"Come outside with me. It's so beautiful out here. I have so much to show you," Miracle said.

Her hands wrapped around my wrist. Tugging gently me to join her outside of my front door.

I couldn't.

The invisible line between being outside under the endless Wyoming sky and inside with my sadness felt like barbed wire. The threshold we were standing in was like thick amber.

I was stuck.

I hated when Miracle showed up like this unannounced at my door. It was really rude. It was presumptuous. It was without any social etiquette.

It was just like her.

"I'd love to go outside with you but I can't," I told Miracle.

She kissed the top of my clenched fists she was still holding on to and asked:

"How come?"

I looked at Miracle and sighed. She was now covered in blue and red butterflies. Her body was a tapestry of little wings opening and closing so deliberately. She smiled at me with lips that had become clouds.

How come??!!

What in the hell kind of question was that? How could she ask me that? Miracle knew the exact reason why I couldn't go outside with her.

John Roedel

It was the same reason I couldn't walk out with her yesterday or the countless days before that when she showed out up to invite me to go with her.

She was going to make me say it out loud. Fine. I would tell her exactly why I couldn't go outside with her. Anything for her to get bored and finally leave me alone for good.

"Because my depression won't let me!" I shouted over the sound of her drumming butterfly wings.

"Why?" she asked.

I was full-on angry now. I ripped my wrist out of her hand and moved to shut the door. Miracle's foot blocked it. I looked into her eyes that had become twin sunsets. They blazed like an endless autumn.

"Why what?" I asked.

"Why do you keep asking your depression for permission to live your life?"

I couldn't find an answer to give her. Which turns out was my answer.

After a moment Miracle blanketed my hand with hers again. It was so warm. I could feel her veins writing a new gospel inside of me as our wrists pressed together. We spent ten minutes crying together and then she pulled on my hand once more - indicating it was time for us to leave.

"Ready to go?" she asked.

I was.

I had always been.

John Roedel

#36

I don't know if this is going
to be a poem or not.

I haven't quite figured it out yet.

So far sure looks like a poem -
   but looks can be deceiving.

Maybe this isn't a poem.
Maybe this is a conversation?

Yes, I think that's exactly what this is.
   This is a conversation between us.

I'm right there with you now.
   I've time-traveled right to you from the past.

I typed my way to the other side of your eyes.
   It's time to say everything unsaid between us.

I've been wanting to ask you
something for a long while now

but I've been afraid to ask
until now

How are you?

Wait. Don't tell me what I want to hear.
   Wait. Don't tell you what you want to hear.

Tell the truth, my love.
There is no right answer.
Just be real —

How are you?

Are you ok?
   It's ok if you aren't. It really is.
Are you happy?

John Roedel

It's ok if you are. It really is.

How are you?

Are you telling your story to the world?
    I hope you are. We all need to hear it.
Are you turning your life into a song?
    I hope you are. We all need to feel it.

How are you?

Have you given your heart to another?
    Laying in the arms of our beloved is magic.
Have you had your heart broken?
    Recovering from heartbreak is also magic.

How are you?

Floating like a wild balloon at sunset?
    Or are you rooted like an ancient elm at dawn?
Are you out there searching for beauty?
    Or are you crying behind locked doors?

How are you?

Has your life turned out how you had hoped?
    Where every breath you take is an adventure.
Or have things unraveled for you?
    And now you're spilled out on the floor.

How are you?

It's been so long since
we've really talked like this.

Have you had a hard time sleeping?

When you close your eyes at night do you only see the faces of
the people who hurt you?

Are there monsters under your bed that growl a litany of your past
sins up to you while you toss and turn under your covers?

John Roedel

Is there a dripping hive of anxiety bees buzzing in your stomach?

Does your heart sound like mysterious drums coming out of a haunted forest?

Does any of that seem familiar?

How are you?

Are you sad all of the time?
Are you still laughing at dirty jokes?
Are you hiding inside wine bottles?
Are you fighting for your dreams?
Are you spending any time watching clouds?
Are you throwing away your wedding album?
Are you getting used to loneliness?
Are you dancing in your sundress?
Are you gossiping with angels?
Are you still mad at the world?
Are you happy with your job?
Are you going back to school?
Are you writing love letters again?
Are you punishing yourself?
Are you kissing with your eyes closed?
Are you dreaming of your escape?
Are you on top of the world?
Are you tying cords around your neck?
Are you laughing at yourself?
Are you on a diet?
Are you having the best sex of your life?
Are you covered in grief?
Are you still writing that book?
Are you keeping secrets?
Are you utterly ruined?
Are you praying for a sign from God?
Are you patient with your kids?
Are you gardening again?
Are you in pieces?
Are you trying on wedding dresses?
Are you waiting for things to get back to normal?
Are you arguing with people online?

John Roedel

Are you redecorating your home?
Are you retiring?
Are you pregnant?
Are you developing an allergy to gluten?
Are you still fishing with live bait?
Are you thinking about death more?
Are you climbing the walls?
 Are you changing your will?
Are you trying to keep your light from dimming?
Are you spending too much on take-out food?
Are you ignoring your texts?
Are you screaming at the sky?
Are you going to counseling?
Are you being romantic?
Are you ever going to forgive them?
Are you punching the clock with sore knuckles?
Are you still waiting for your turn?
Are you able to look at the mirror?
Are you planning your next vacation?
Are you chewing your nails?
Are you filled with joy?
Are you reaping what you sow?
Are you part of the solution?
Are you depressed?
Are you twisting in the wind?
Are you begging for scraps?
Are you still singing in the shower?
Are you questioning everything?
Are you ever going to come home again?
Are you itching your scars?
Are you still skinny dipping in lakes?
Are you making the best of it?
Are you giving up on me?
Are you deciding which way you are going?
Are you forgiving them?
Are you sobbing on park benches?
Are you allowing room for hope?
Are you wrestling with demons?
Are you sunbathing in meadows?
Are you still feeling phantom pains?
Are you advocating for yourself?

John Roedel

Are you going to let them off the hook?
Are you finger painting on walls?
Are you lying to strangers?
Are you opening the curtains?
Are you betting on yourself?
Are you ever going to love again?
Are you thinking about hurting yourself?
Are you running for office?
Are you worrying about bills?
Are you giggling with besties?
Are you still drinking too much coffee?
Are you shopping for satin sheets?
Are you nostalgic for your childhood?
Are you hiding a hickey?
Are you trying to give up sugar?
Are you and God on a break?
Are you the envy of others?
Are you creating burner Instagram accounts?
Are you going back to basics?
Are you going to ever try mediation?
Are you feeling empty inside?
Are you getting that promotion?
Are you going to tell anyone about that bruise?
Are you dreading going on that date?
Are you having nightmares still?
Are you obsessed with the news?
Are you asking for help?
Are you at peace?
Are you looking for a new community?
Are you going to let yourself be a little reckless?
Are you getting yours?
Are you still unfolding your life map?
Are you ever going to tell me your secret?
Are you reading smutty books?
Are you weaving flowers in your hair?
Are you saving the world?
Are you just getting by?

Tell me. Please.
How are you?

John Roedel

After you do - it will be my turn
to tell you something.

And it's this -

whatever your storm is
whatever your season is
whatever your sorrow is
whatever your success is
whatever your sin is
whatever your song is
whatever your sadness is
whatever your sweetness is

whatever your whatever is

embrace it
   feel every moment of it

                the good
             the terrible
              the blah
        the redemption
         the numbness
            the hope
         the heartache
         the mourning
          the laughter
            the rage
        the loneliness
            the pain
             the joy
        the seductive
         the anxiety
        the gentleness
         the certainty
          the doubt
           the cold
         the weight
       the forgiveness
           the love
       the exhaustion

John Roedel

and the fire
the fire
the fire - oh my love,
especially the fire

feel it all
every. single. bit. of. it.

because that is what this whole experiment is about
- it's about feeling

don't hide from it

when you're worried - let yourself be worried
when you're silly - let yourself be silly
when you're furious- let yourself be furious
when you're amazing - let yourself be amazing
when you're broken- let yourself be broken

don't shut it in
don't deny it

what you're feeling
   what you're experiencing
what you're going through
   is worthy of your attention

sometimes we bury our lives
   under the dirt fake smiles
      and peat moss of "fitting in"

there's no time for that anymore
   in this, the age of raw authenticity.

So, my love, let me ask again

how are you?

before you answer that to yourself
   let me just say one more thing before
I skip through the screen
   and back in time.

John Roedel

I told you that this likely wasn't
   going to be a poem.

I was right - this isn't a poem.

You are the poem
   everything about you is poetry.

the way you look behind candlelight
the way you rise like steam every morning
the way you brush your hair from your eyes
the way you recover from your failures
the way you refuse to give up after heartbreak
the way you hold your hands to keep them from shaking
the way you fight for what you believe in
the way you accidentally snort when you laugh
the way you became more than your mistakes
the way that you glide into a room

everything you do is the poem
   You are the poetry

and the most beautiful verses of you
are your emotions

They are the lyrics of your soul
   -your lovely, untamed and burning soul.

and when you share your feelings
the world stands still
and I hold my breath
and the ground splits open
and I fall straight into the tear-soaked pages
of your authenticity

please don't be ashamed
   to speak so true that the paint
runs off the wall and down your face

   -color this room in your feelings

John Roedel

It's time.
  Take a deep breath.

My love,
  please please please please
tell me

how are you?

John Roedel

#37

would you do me a favor?

can you love yourself
for just ten seconds?

can you love yourself
no matter what

the marks in your arms that you
gave yourself yesterday

or what the cruel words he said
that has now nested in your ears?

can you love yourself
despite

the image your crooked mirror
reflects back at you

or the stack of yellowing bills
on your counter

the fresh clump of hair
resting on your shower drain?

can you love yourself
even though

you now have matching holes in your
favorite shirt and heart

and fresh creases in your face that
weren't there yesterday?

can you love yourself
no matter what

the scale in
your bathroom

John Roedel

says about you?

can you just love yourself
for ten seconds?

that's it
just ten seconds

please don't shake your head

take my hand

and take
just ten seconds
to remember

how lovely you are

that's it
ten seconds

go ahead and give it a try

take a deep breath
I'll count for you

———————————

1
your name is the first word of somebody's favorite sentence

2
you are the trembling cocoon - just ready to burst into colors
nobody else has ever seen before

3
you are perfect right now as you are - yes, you are - yes, you are
perfect right now - your scars are what make you beautiful

4

John Roedel

your tears are shaped like seeds for a reason - they are growing
your new Eden one drop at a time

5

the holes in you have become a wind instrument that plays your
redemption song

6

you are not your past crimes, sins, mistakes or failures - you are
the rising fire - you are the resurrected heartbeat - you are the
reborn tigress - you are the reclamation of purpose - you are the
baptismal river - you are the same untouched soul that you were
on your very first day - you are still who you were born to be

7

you are a sunflower growing in the cracked sidewalk

8

you are what angels write poetry about in the trees

9

you are in the middle of your story - this isn't your end - this is just
the part in the story where you face the dragon - this despair you
are feeling is limited to this page - there are so many pages to
come - there are so many new words ready for you to read - each
page of your story smells like morning rain - there is so much of
your story left to be told - your final chapter will someday be
called "How I Became a Wind Chime in The Storm"

10
you are eternal
you are eternal
you are eternal

everything else
is temporary

you will outlive your fears
you will outlast your anxieties
you will outrun your suffering

John Roedel

when everything that is troubling you reached its expiration date -
you will keep going

you were lit long ago
to never be put out

everything else
is temporary

you are eternal
you are eternal
you are eternal

_____

there!

we made it ten seconds

could you love yourself
for that long?

I know it's hard
but
can we try again?

this time
you count
to ten

and with every second
remember the truth

of who you are

and what you were
created to be

and say it out loud
and honor your existence

and fall in love with yourself

John Roedel

all over again

my hands are shaking too

let's try counting to ten again

1 yo
2 u
3 ar
4 e
5 so so so
6 be
7 au
8 ti
9 fu
10 l

John Roedel

#38

on my last day
here on Earth
let me be as I
was on my very
first day

let me be

ready for my
great voyage
between worlds

let me ready
to ride the cosmic
river of the vast unknown

on my last day
here on Earth
let me be as I
was on my very first

let me be

ready to see what
all the fuss is on
the other side of
the womb that I've been
hearing so much about

let me be

ready to be bathed in
a light that I could have
never have imagined

let me be

ready to be held in
the arms by my lovely
creator and to feel safer

John Roedel

than I ever have before

on my last day
here on Earth
let me be as I
was on my very first

let me be

ready to see the smiling faces
of all those who have been
eagerly waiting to meet me

let me be

ready to be swaddled up
in the warmest cotton
blanket of fresh starts

on my last day
here on Earth
let me be as
I was on my very first

covered in the
miracle of creation

no wonder newborn
babies cry

no wonder 45-year old
men cry
it's all such an adventure
it's all such a journey
it's all such a circle
it's all such a flowing river

it's all such an endless passage
it's all such a mystery

and it goes on and on and on
and on and on

John Roedel

it all goes on

and we go on and on and on
and on and on

we all go on

oh, divine light
oh, sacred spirit
oh, God

please let me

go on and on and on
and on and on

oh, I can't wait to see
what comes next

John Roedel

#39

my love,
take your time
to heal

the way back to yourself
isn't a breathless race

or a runaway train

your rehabilitation
requires respite

not rush

our rustic open wounds
become symmetrically
formed scars when we
allow ourselves time to rest

not when we thrash around

- the way to healing isn't a mountain
that you must scale

- your recovery isn't a barrier
that you have to climb

- your comeback isn't an
obstacle course

of dangling legs,
grasping fingers
or racing heartbeats
that you are being called
to scramble around,
across or through

you won't mend
your heart

John Roedel

by "getting over"
what happened to you

your suffering isn't a
rickety ladder
of noisy steps

- it's a quiet church of whispering angels
- it's a still lake of your beautiful reflection
- it's a sacred school house of learning

if we don't spend time with
our pain

we never learn from it

if we don't listen to the shifting
deep rumbles inside of us

we will build our lives on fault lines

if we treat our trauma like a
racecourse to speed through

we will keep crashing into the walls

I don't believe you
will ever "get over"
anything terrible that
has happened to you

like it is a fence

instead

I believe that if
you rest with your pain
under a tree for an
hour or two

like it is your best friend

John Roedel

it will remind you
over and over about

how you are your most
beautiful when you refuse to give up

don't let them lie to
you when they tell
you to "move on"
from your wounds

your wounds
make the best
teachers

they have so
much to teach you
about the wealth
of courage you
have inside of you

your pain isn't
an obstacle
it's an open court testimony
of how remarkably
brave you are

when you want to
know peace again

after you fall
to pieces
don't speed through
your recovery

lie down with your
fat tears on
the couch
for as long as
it takes
to remember

John Roedel

there is absolutely nothing
that can stop you

you don't need
to overcome anything
like it is a wall

you just need to rest
for a bit
and that's how you
come back to yourself again

- one long nap at a time

my love,
take your time
to heal

I'll be here waiting
for you to emerge
from under the
blankets like the
Rose of Advent

I'll be here writing
poetry about how
brave you are to
keep breathing

I'll be here marveling
at how lovely you are
when you wear your scars
like midnight lingerie

John Roedel

#40

I was born with a last name
and all the expectations that
came with it

from birth, I was crafted
to be an origami swan

to have perfectly folded edges
to exist on a shelf
to be looked at from a distance
to appear complete
to live precisely

I tried to live that way
- I swear I did

even during the days
when I could feel the exact
geometry inside of me
start to become wild poetry

I would resist the urge to
let go of the form
I was told to live by
if I wanted to be happy

I stayed as folded
as I could
despite the growing
sound of crinkling paper
coming from inside of my
loose leaf heart

one morning - not too long ago

I woke up and I noticed that my perfectly
shaped swan wings had a wrinkle in it

I tried to hide my imperfection
from the world by only letting

John Roedel

people see my good side

my faultless side
my seamless side

a short while later I noticed
that my other wing had lost
its tight fold and was curling outward

I was coming
undone and unfolded
right in front of the world

the rest of me
started falling
apart soon after

within a short time
I no longer looked
like a perfect swan

I had become a flattened out piece
of paper with more crows-feet
creases in my firm than I could count

eventually, a breeze came
and took me off of my shelf
to carry me out of the window
and into the untamed wild

it was that moment when
I was my most unfurled self
that I called out to God

"where are my perfect folds?
where have my straight lines gone?"
I asked the empty sky

God spouted out of the ground
next to me in the form of a wildflower

"they are gone, my love,

John Roedel

all those things you once
thought you were are now gone"

I cried

"why are you crying?" God asked while stretching out above me
with flower petals of at least a half-dozen colors that had never
seen before from the safe shelf I had lived most of my life from.

"because without my folds and lines that I was given I have no
purpose," I sobbed. "Without my hard edges and defined creases,
I don't know who I am anymore."

"I do," God said while exploding into an Easter bloom.

I held my breath.

"You finally get to be you. You are now an untouched canvas who
decides what it gets to be marked with. You are lucky enough to
be a piece of blank paper that gets to choose what is written on
it. You get to be a selection of art that you get to help create. You
are now able to leave behind the expectations this world has for
you to be perfect - and now you get to become whatever you want
to be."

God was now a towering wildflower that was riding up to kiss the
sun.

"Oh," I replied while looking at myself with new eyes.

Instead of being tightly bound together, I was now an
outstretched creation. Instead of being a perfect sculpture, I was
an open hand.

"What now?" I asked the wildflower of God.

"What now?" God laughed. "Anything. Everything. It's all in front of
you. It's all adventure from here."

Suddenly a gust of wind picked me up

John Roedel

again and started carrying me to the horizon.

Even though I had been a swan my whole life the first time I ever flew was when I lost my wings.

I smiled.

What an adventure it is to come undone.

John Roedel

Epilogue #1

When we say
"I have depression."

what you seem to hear is
"I'm fragile."

-There is nothing fragile about us.

-We are the weathered seaside cliff that
has survived a century of crashing waves
and well-meaning stomping tourists
who only came to visit to see if the
ancient lighthouse on top of us still works

-We are the bright wildflower that somehow
finds a way to push itself up through the
cracked and dirty sidewalk outside of
your apartment building

-We are the blind songbirds who still
finds the perfect lyrics to their hymn at sunrise
despite the fact they don't know what
the breaking dawn looks like

-We are the heart born with a gaping hole
in the center of it that we have turned into
a wind chime to signal to the world that
we are more than a murmur

-We are the wandering ghosts in your
house banging on the walls every night
until the bridge of light we have been looking
for reveals itself to us

-We are the grief-stricken comedians
who have fashioned their suffering into
a hammer that they use to hit your
funny bone with

-We are the miners who have spent

John Roedel

the better part of their lives digging
through deep dark caves in search
of a long lost hidden vein of mercy

-We are the last orange leaf
on the bare elm that refuses
to give into the chew of winter because
spring is always just a single warm breath away

- We are the clouds above you that
keep molding, breaking, shapeshifting
into whatever we need to look like
in order to make it to the next horizon

- We are the broken pieces of an
ornamental vase that has
been glued back together with
wabi-sabi gold to make us beautiful

- We are the winter-ravaged
tree that will contort itself
into whatever shape that will
keep it from snapping in two

- We are the war-torn church
who is adorned in bullet holes
and in ruby red stained glass
in equal measure

We are not fragile

We are the incomplete - yet whole
We are the lost - yet purposeful

We are the rubble - and the garden
We are the besieged - and the hopeful

We are the rocks in the
rapids that have been polished

We are the sin and the redemption

John Roedel

We have learned to grow fruit trees
in a shadowland of obscured light
and hungry vultures

We have screamed into the bathroom tiles until
our voices turn themselves into a crutch
that we use to lift ourselves back up

We will fight like hell
to stay here with you on Earth
no matter the invisible knife
that's been twisting in our stomach
for years

- we are the rainbow amid the tempest

and there isn't a single thing
fragile about us

John Roedel

Epilogue #2

I had insomnia
last night

so I went outside
and stood barefoot
in the Wyoming snow

it was so cold that
the moonlight
froze in my hair

like little strands
of glowing cotton candy

that's exactly when I heard
a gravelly voice from
right behind me

it was the voice of fear

"You aren't ever going to be okay,"
fear said to me in her
trademark smoker's rasp

"Maybe," I replied.
"But I'm still here
and I'm still fighting."

"I hate how you use that word," fear groaned

"Which word is that?" I asked

"Still" fear said.

"Oh."

With that the moon
above us became
a campfire

John Roedel

and the snow around
my feet melted

and my fear sunk
into a puddle

and the once frozen
moonlight in my
hair ran down my face
like fat juicy baptismal tears

and it did, in fact, [OBJ]
taste just
like cotton candy

and I smiled for
the first time
in a year

and I haven't stopped

because I'm
still here

still
still
still
here

and so are you

despite everything
you've been asked
to endure

- you remain

all the fear
all the despair
all the setbacks

couldn't stop you

John Roedel